COZUMEL TRAVEL GUIDE FOR BEGINNERS

The Updated Concise Guide for Planning a Trip to Cozumel Including Top Destinations,Culture,Outdoor Adventures,Dining,Cuisine and Getting Around

Nicolash Enzo
Copyright@2023

TABLE OF CONTENT

CHAPTER 1

INTRODUCTION

Situated inside the turquoise waters of the Caribbean Sea, Cozumel serves as a dynamic and captivating addition to Mexico's array of sought-after tourist locations. This beautiful island, characterized by its unspoiled beaches, fascinating marine biodiversity, and significant cultural legacy, provides an ideal combination of leisure and exploration for all those that arrive on its coast. Cozumel has gained recognition for its notable coral reefs, varied marine habitats, and welcoming hospitality, making it a highly sought-after destination for those interested in nature and recreational activities.

An Extraordinary Geographic Phenomenon

Cozumel, with a land size of over 480 square kilometers, stands as the most expansive inhabited island inside the nation of Mexico. Located in close proximity to the eastern coast of the Yucatán Peninsula, it is situated in direct opposition to the well-known Riviera Maya. The strategic positioning of this area has significantly influenced its development as a prosperous tourism attraction. The island's increased visibility on the worldwide tourist landscape may be attributed to its convenient accessibility through the Cozumel International Airport and its status as a favored destination for cruise ships.

An Oasis for Tourists

Cozumel extends a warm invitation to anyone seeking to transcend the mundane and indulge in a realm of captivating tropical charm. The island's appeal goes beyond its aesthetic qualities, including a convergence of historical significance, cultural richness, and opportunities for thrilling experiences. The immaculate coastlines, adorned with fine-grained white sand and caressed by the tranquil Caribbean tides, provide an enticing setting for engaging in sunbathing, swimming, and unwinding by the seaside. Palancar Beach exemplifies the distinctive coastal allure of Cozumel with its scenic backdrop and pristine seas. Paradise Beach, as its name suggests, provides a captivating combination of lively water activities and serene sunsets that mesmerize tourists with their inherent beauty.

Exploring the Depths: An Enchanting Subaquatic Realm

The beaches of Cozumel exhibit remarkable beauty, although it is in its underwater realm that the true enchantment unfolds. The island has exceptionally clear seas that harbor a multitude of different and awe-inspiring coral reefs, ranking among the most biodiverse globally. The seas in question attract snorkeling and scuba diving enthusiasts from all parts of the world who want to see the vibrant array of colors shown by the coral reefs. The Palancar Reef is well recognized as a prominent destination for diving enthusiasts, renowned for its captivating array of coral formations and diverse marine ecosystem. Its intricate maze-like structure and abundant marine life have a profound and enduring impact on the individuals lucky enough to go into its profound depths. Both the Santa Rosa Wall and Columbia Reef exhibit a fascinating allure, as they unveil the marvels of the marine realm via their complex ecosystems and flourishing aquatic organisms.

The presence of remnants from a bygone society

In addition to its picturesque beaches and inviting seas, Cozumel has a profound cultural legacy that echoes the narratives of a bygone civilisation. The island was once regarded as a consecrated location devoted to the veneration of Ixchel, the Maya deity associated with fertility. The San Gervasio Ruins, an archaeological site located in the central region of Cozumel, provide valuable insights into the profound spiritual importance that the Maya people attributed to the island. The vestiges of architectural constructions and ceremonial hubs provide an opportunity to glimpse into historical periods, enabling visitors to be transported to an era when the island served

An Exploration of Culinary Harmonies

The island's appeal beyond its aesthetic charm and historical importance, including a gastronomic experience of exceptional quality. The dining scene in Cozumel showcases a harmonious blend of traditional Mexican flavors and global culinary influences, presenting a diverse selection of meals that cater to a wide range of tastes. Cozumel's dining experiences include a diverse range of culinary offerings, showcasing the island's coastal setting via delicious seafood specialties and providing visitors opportunity to savor the original flavors of Mexican cuisine at colorful street food stalls.

These gastronomic encounters serve as a festival of culinary talent, highlighting the skill and creativity of the local chefs.

The subject of this discourse is an island that offers a plethora of thrilling experiences and activities.

The allure of Cozumel extends beyond opportunities for leisure and discovery, including a rich array of adventurous experiences. Opportunities for exhilarating adventures await beyond the glistening seas. ATV trips provide individuals with the opportunity to go on off-road expeditions into verdant rainforests and challenging landscapes, so affording them a unique vantage point from which to appreciate the island's inherent beauty. In contrast, Jeep safaris provide a comprehensive encounter that integrates both exploration and instruction, giving participants the opportunity to acquire knowledge about the many ecosystems, plant life, and animal species found on the island.

Strategizing Your Cozumel Getaway

When embarking on a visit to Cozumel, it is important to take into account the climatic conditions of the island. The period from November to April, known as the dry season, is often considered the most favorable time for visiting due to the consistently great weather conditions that are conducive to engaging in outdoor activities. The official currency used in the region is the Mexican Peso. Although several businesses do take major credit cards, it is recommended to have a certain amount of cash on hand for transactions at smaller locations.

Prior to embarking on a journey, it is advisable to acquaint oneself with the norms and traditions of the local community in order to guarantee a visit that is characterized by respect and cultural sensitivity. Although Spanish serves as the official language, English is often used in tourist regions, hence facilitating communication for foreign visitors.

In summary, Cozumel presents a unique amalgamation of natural phenomena, cultural abundance, and thrilling encounters. Cozumel offers a transformative experience that beyond the mundane, leaving a lasting impression on one's emotions, whether via deep-sea diving, archaeological expeditions, or the appreciation of its culinary delights. Prepare your belongings, fully engage with the aesthetic appeal of the island, and let the captivating allure of Cozumel to gradually reveal itself to you.

CHAPTER 2

Getting to Cozumel

Cozumel, an island renowned for its tranquil natural landscapes and exhilarating recreational opportunities, beckons tourists to explore its captivating allure situated in the central region of the Caribbean Sea. This tropical destination entices visitors with its pristine seas, abundant natural beauty, and cultural heritage, which can be easily accessed via a range of transportation options. Regardless of the mode of transportation chosen, whether it air or water, the voyage to Cozumel has a crucial role in shaping the whole encounter, establishing the ambiance for the captivating allure that awaits.

Title: A Comprehensive Analysis of Aerial Pathways: The Case of Cozumel International Airport Introduction: This study aims to provide a comprehensive analysis of the aerial pathways associated with Cozumel International Airport. By examining the many aspects of

The Cozumel International Airport serves as a convenient and efficient gateway for those who prioritize the expediency of air transportation. The contemporary airport facility accommodates both international and local aircraft, so facilitating convenient access for guests from many regions to this idyllic island destination. Cozumel, as a destination, benefits from a robust network of airlines that provide frequent flights, connecting North America, Europe, and other regions.

Upon arrival, individuals are met with a combination of contemporary amenities and a kind reception from the local Mexican community. The airport's operational efficiency and provision of services that cater to the needs of passengers contribute to a seamless transition from air travel to the coastlines of the island. Located in close proximity to the airport, a short drive gives access to a range of hotels on the island, enabling tourists to promptly establish themselves in their preferred refuge and begin their exploration endeavors.

The topic of discussion is Sailing into Splendor: Cruise Ships and Port Facilities.

The allure of Cozumel goes beyond its airport. Additionally, it is well recognized as a prominent destination for several cruise vessels that traverse the pristine seas of the Caribbean. The island's port facilities, due to its strategic location, are much sought after as a stop on several cruise itineraries, providing guests with the opportunity to experience a plethora of tropical pleasures.

As the cruise ships get nearer to the island, the picturesque shoreline of Cozumel gradually becomes visible, like a surreal vision on the far horizon. The port's efficacy in managing marine traffic facilitates a seamless disembarkation procedure, enabling guests to promptly set foot on the island's terrain and experience its allure. The port area serves as a representative sample of the many attractions available in Cozumel, including a range of establishments such as stores, restaurants, and activities that provide insight into the island's lively cultural milieu.

Exploring Maritime Transportation: Ferries Departing from Playa del Carmen

A frequently chosen and visually appealing transportation method for those already situated in the Riviera Maya area is to use a ferry service that operates between Playa del Carmen and Cozumel. The voyage across the Caribbean Sea exemplifies the magnificence of the natural world, as individuals are presented with awe-inspiring panoramas of the azure seas and the far-off horizon.

Ferries provide a diverse selection of alternatives, including both conventional passenger ferries and high-speed catamarans. The voyage itself becomes an integral component of the expedition, affording passengers the opportunity to experience the refreshing ocean wind, bask in the soothing rays of the sun, and fully engage with the serene atmosphere that characterizes the Caribbean region.

Upon arrival at the beaches of Cozumel, passengers are greeted with a vibrant boat port that exudes a lively atmosphere. The terminal's amenities guarantee a smooth and uninterrupted transfer experience, offering a range of services that cater to the various requirements of passengers, such as giving information on nearby points of interest and available ground transportation alternatives.

Selecting Your Journey: Customizing Your Arrival Encounter

Cozumel has a variety of alternatives to accommodate diverse interests and travel patterns, regardless of whether visitors arrive by flight, cruise ship, or ferry. The selection of the mode of arrival encompasses not just considerations of convenience, but also aims to establish a lasting and engaging encounter from the first moment that individual steps onto the island.

The Cozumel International Airport offers a convenient means of aerial transportation for anyone seeking a prompt and effective transfer. This enables passengers to expeditiously arrive at their chosen lodgings and start their exploration of Cozumel.

On the contrary, those who have a strong interest in cruises are provided with a distinctive combination of sea exhilaration and tropical leisure. The port facilities on the island function as a primary entry point to the many attractions and local culture of Cozumel, providing visitors with a condensed experience that encapsulates the essence of the island's character.

For those who choose a more relaxed and visually appealing means of transportation, the boat voyage originating from Playa del Carmen is a chance to establish a connection with the immense expanse of the ocean and admire the splendor of the Caribbean Sea.

Embracing the Warm Reception of Cozumel Island

The transportation to Cozumel, whether by air or boat, is a fundamental component of the total experience. Upon the arrival of guests to this captivating island, they are not only welcomed by its aesthetically pleasing landscape, but also by the prospect of exploration, excitement, and rejuvenation.

The routes of arrival in Cozumel accommodate many travel preferences, enabling guests to customize their itineraries and establish the desired ambiance for the next days of tranquility. Regardless of the chosen course, the expectation of fully engaging with the captivating attraction of Cozumel imbues the expedition with the essence of a preliminary stage leading to an indelible getaway.

CHAPTER 3

Top Attractions in Cozumel

Cozumel, an island located in the Caribbean Sea, is a highly sought-after destination that captivates the interest and affections of global tourists. Cozumel is well recognized for its unspoiled beaches, diverse marine ecosystem, and significant cultural legacy, offering a stunning assortment of activities that guarantee indelible encounters. The island's prominent attractions include a diverse range of experiences, blending elements of adventure, awe, and discovery, from the deep depths of its pristine seas to the vestiges of bygone civilizations.

1. Cozumel's Beaches: Serene Escapes of Tranquility

The coastline of Cozumel exhibits remarkable natural beauty, showcasing a collection of enticing beaches that are renowned in the Caribbean region. Every beach exhibits its own distinct allure, providing an enticing retreat for those in search of tranquility, aquatic activities, or a romantic evening promenade.

Playa Palancar is a renowned beach destination. Playa Palancar allures visitors with its picturesque features, characterized by its pristine white sand and tranquil azure seas, reminiscent of a surreal dream-like setting. This beach offers a peaceful and calm environment, encouraging tourists to relax under the gently swaying palm palms, enjoy tropical beverages, and appreciate the exquisite natural scenery. Snorkeling and kayaking are widely favored recreational pursuits in this locale, affording enthusiasts the opportunity to engage in the exploration of the diverse marine ecosystem situated in close proximity to the beach.

Paradise Beach is a renowned coastal destination known for its scenic beauty and recreational opportunities. Paradise Beach lives up to its name by embodying the essence of an idyllic paradise. This multifaceted location is ideal for anyone seeking both tranquility and exhilaration. One may engage in leisurely activities such as reclining on the comfortable sandy beach, immersing oneself in the alluring aquatic environment, or partaking in thrilling water-based recreational pursuits such as jet skiing and parasailing. As the diurnal cycle progresses towards dusk, behold the sun's resplendent dip below the celestial boundary, bestowing a captivating aura onto the shoreline and its occupants.

The Chankanaab Beach Adventure Park is a notable destination that offers a range of recreational activities and attractions for visitors to enjoy. In addition to its visually captivating natural surroundings, Chankanaab Beach Adventure Park provides a diverse array of amenities and activities that are suitable for individuals of all ages, ensuring an inclusive experience for families. Engage in snorkeling activities within the unspoiled waters, investigate the submerged sculptures, or go in a relaxed swim inside the naturally occurring lagoon. The botanical garden inside the park serves as a sanctuary characterized by abundant vegetation, providing a tranquil haven for anyone in need of solace from the sun's rays.

2. Snorkeling and Diving Sites: An Access Point to an Enchanting Subaquatic Realm

The marine assets of Cozumel transcend its coastal boundaries, offering an enticing opportunity for anyone to engage in an immersive experience inside a realm characterized by lively coral reefs, diverse fish species, and captivating undersea phenomena.

Palancar Reef, a prominent attraction on the island, has significant value and is highly recommended for both snorkelers and divers. The complex arrangements of coral and diverse marine organisms have established its standing as a globally recognized destination for diving enthusiasts. Divers submerge into a vibrant and ecologically diverse environment, where they come across marine turtles, rays, and a variety of tropical fish species.

The Santa Rosa Wall is a prominent structure that is the focus of this discussion. Santa Rosa Wall is an exemplary manifestation of natural architecture, characterized by its remarkable vertical descent into substantial depths. The submerged environment in question is characterized by an array of colorful corals and sponges, which provide as a visually captivating setting for interactions with a diverse range of marine organisms, varying in their physical forms and dimensions.

Columbia Reef is a geographical feature that will be discussed in this academic text. The Columbia Reef is characterized by a diverse array of brilliant colors and a bustling ecosystem of marine life. The flow of water in this particular area exerts a magnetic pull on several groups of fish, resulting in a visually captivating display characterized by dynamic movement and a vibrant array of hues. Divers has the ability to traverse tunnels and canyons, hence facilitating the exploration of the complicated structures present in the reef. During these expeditions, divers may come across many marine species, including eels, nurse sharks, and sometimes, hammerhead sharks.

3. The Mayan Ruins: Traces of an Ancient Civilization The Mayan ruins serve as remnants of a once-thriving ancient civilization, offering valuable insights into their culture, architecture, and societal practices. These archaeological sites provide a glimpse into the rich history and legacy of the Mayan people, allowing us to

The charm of Cozumel extends beyond its aesthetic appeal, including a rich historical and cultural heritage. The Mayan ruins found on the island provide an opportunity to get insight into the historical culture that flourished in this region.

The San Gervasio Ruins are a significant archaeological site. San Gervasio, a collection of buildings, serves as a pilgrimage destination devoted to the veneration of the Mayan goddess of fertility. This sacred location possessed great spiritual importance in ancient times. One may traverse the remnants of ancient structures and encounter the vestiges of temples and altars, establishing a profound connection with the historical significance of the island as a renowned site of religious veneration.

El Cedral is a historical site located on the Mexican island of Cozumel. El Cedral serves as a tangible manifestation of the historical evolution of the island, symbolizing its progression from a modest settlement to a prosperous tourist attraction.

The El Cedral Church, a renowned architectural structure constructed during the 16th century, serves as a testament to the historical development of Cozumel. The yearly celebration held at the location is commemorated via lively parades and customary dances, serving as a tribute to the island's rich cultural legacy.

The Cozumel Museum: Revealing the Narrative of the Island

The Cozumel Museum offers a wealth of information for anybody interested in gaining a more profound comprehension of the history and culture of Cozumel. The displays inside the museum provide a comprehensive account of the island's development, including its geological origins and its notable role within the Mayan civilisation. The exhibition of captivating antiques, educational displays, and engaging interactive exhibits provides a thorough insight into the historical and contemporary aspects of Cozumel.

5. Punta Sur Eco Beach Park: A Sanctuary for Nature The Punta Sur Eco Beach Park is a remarkable destination that serves as a sanctuary for the preservation and appreciation of nature.

The Punta Sur Eco Beach Park is renowned for its abundant natural variety and awe-inspiring panoramic views. The park in question is characterized by its vast expanse, which includes many natural features such as beaches, lagoons, and dense rainforests. It provides a diverse array of activities that facilitate a meaningful connection between tourists and the surrounding natural environment. Visitors have the opportunity to climb the renowned Celarain Lighthouse, renowned for its historical significance, in order to get a comprehensive vantage point of the island and its environs. Alternatively, individuals may choose to partake in a guided boat excursion to explore the park's intricate lagoon system. The park's dedication to conservation and the promotion of sustainable tourism makes it a very desirable location for environmentally aware tourists.

6. Dolphin Discovery Cozumel: An Interactive Experience with Dolphins

Dolphin Discovery Cozumel provides a unique and noteworthy chance for anyone to engage with highly intelligent aquatic organisms within a respectful and educational environment. Visitors have the opportunity to engage in swimming, recreational activities, and educational experiences centered on dolphins, fostering a unique bond with these docile animals. The aforementioned contact not only facilitates a transcendental experience, but also serves to foster consciousness and admiration for the preservation of marine life.

The vast array of attractions in Cozumel serves as evidence of the island's capacity to accommodate a wide variety of interests and preferences. The island's attractions include a diverse range of captivating features, including sun-drenched beaches, undersea marvels, cultural treasures, and educational opportunities. Cozumel extends a warm invitation to those with a variety of interests, including those who like beaches, history, adventure, and nature. This destination offers a wealth of treasures to explore and opportunities to create lasting experiences that will last even after departing from its coastal region. As one embarks on the Cozumel trip, they may anticipate being enthralled by the island's aesthetic appeal, cultural richness, and the potential for novel revelations at every juncture.

CHAPTER 4

Outdoor Activities

Cozumel, renowned for its breathtaking scenery and mesmerizing bodies of water, entices those with a penchant for outdoor activities to engage in a voyage of discovery and invigoration. The tropical destination under consideration serves as a hub for many adventurous pursuits, providing a wide range of outdoor activities that facilitate guests in establishing a connection with the natural environment, pushing their own boundaries, and forming enduring recollections. Cozumel's array of outdoor activities include both aquatic adventures and terrestrial expeditions, showcasing a remarkable diversity that is matched only by the exhilaration they provide.

1. Aquatic Sports: Exploring the Domain of Water

Snorkeling is a recreational activity that involves immersing oneself in the captivating beauty of the underwater world.

The pristine waters of Cozumel serve as an entry point to a vibrant undersea ecosystem abundant with diverse marine life and a kaleidoscope of colors. Engaging in snorkeling is an essential pastime that offers individuals with varying degrees of expertise the opportunity to see the captivating marine phenomena concealed under the water's surface. Palancar Reef, Santa Rosa Wall, and Columbia Reef are well recognized snorkeling destinations that allow tourists the opportunity to engage in aquatic activities amid a diverse array of brilliant corals, lively fish species, and even elegant sea turtles. Guided excursions provide valuable opportunities to get a deeper understanding of marine ecosystems, enriching the whole experience via the expertise of knowledgeable guides.

Scuba diving is an activity that involves exploring the depths of the ocean, allowing individuals to uncover enigmatic phenomena and phenomena that lie under the surface.

Cozumel is well recognized as a prominent destination for anyone with a keen interest in scuba diving, since it offers enough opportunities for in-depth exploration and immersion in this recreational activity. The island's renowned coral reefs and steep underwater cliffs provide an exceptional and unequaled opportunity for exploring the marine environment. The Palancar Caves, renowned for their complex formations, and Punta Tunich, notable for their striking coral formations, are a few of the many diving sites that provide captivating opportunities to see marine life. Cozumel's diving sites are designed to accommodate divers of many levels of expertise, including both beginners and seasoned professionals.

Fishing Excursions: An Exploration of Angling in the Caribbean

The island of Cozumel has a diverse marine habitat that encompasses a wide range of fishing options. Fishing expeditions provide anglers the opportunity to throw their hooks into the abundant waters of the Caribbean, with the aim of capturing a diverse array of fish species. Cozumel's fishing charters provide a true representation of island life, offering a range of experiences like as deep-sea fishing for marlin, sailfish, and dorado, as well as leisurely reef fishing expeditions targeting snapper and grouper.

2. Land Expeditions: An Exploration of the Aesthetics of Nature

Exploring Jungle Trails via ATV Tours

For individuals in search of a terrestrial expedition, engaging in ATV trips is an exhilarating method to investigate the natural topography of Cozumel. The guided excursions provide participants with captivating experiences as they go through verdant rainforests, challenging terrains, and unexplored treasures nestled inside the island's core. Engage in the exploration of off-road pathways, see the rich variety of plant and animal life, and experience the exhilarating sensation of adventure, all while fully immersing oneself in the complex ecology of the island.

Jeep Safaris: An Integration of Educational and Exploratory Elements

Jeep safaris provide a unique amalgamation of adventure and educational opportunities, giving guests the chance to traverse Cozumel's many landscapes while acquiring knowledge about its ecosystems and cultural legacy. Embark on a journey through densely vegetated tropical forests, explore the ancient remnants of Mayan civilization, and unveil the concealed cenotes, natural sinkholes, scattered over the island. These safaris provide individuals the chance to engage with the island's inherent aesthetic appeal as well as its profound historical importance.

Zip-Lining: An Aerial Adventure Above the Canopy

Cozumel's zip-lining adventures provide individuals with an opportunity to engage in an exhilarating activity that involves ascending to great heights. By participating in this activity, individuals are afforded a unique perspective from above, allowing them to see and appreciate the abundant flora and picturesque coastline landscapes that adorn the island. Experience the sensation of ascending above the canopy of trees, perceive the exhilarating gusts of wind on your visage, and behold the expansive vistas that extend from the azure lakes to the lush rainforests. Zip-line courses often include both excitement and educational components, offering valuable perspectives on the ecology and wildlife of the island.

Kayaking and paddleboarding are recreational activities that involve navigating serene coastal environments.

The tranquil seas of Cozumel provide an optimal environment for engaging in kayaking and paddleboarding activities, hence giving a peaceful means of exploring the island's coastal regions. Experience the serene motion across the undisturbed ocean, immerse oneself in the radiant rays of sunlight, and appreciate the vivid array of aquatic organisms observable inside the transparent depths. Numerous beach clubs and tour companies provide the convenience of equipment rentals and guided excursions, so guaranteeing a secure and pleasurable experience for all participants.

Beach Volleyball and Games: An Enjoyable Outdoor Activity

The beaches of Cozumel serve as both tranquil retreats and lively gathering places for recreational activities and social bonding. Participate in amicable beach volleyball matches, construct sandcastles with cherished companions, or alternatively, relax and decompress underneath a beach umbrella while engrossed in a literary masterpiece. The beach clubs on the island often arrange events and games, providing opportunities for tourists to engage in social interactions and make enduring memories.

Horseback riding along the coast offers a captivating experience characterized by its elegant ambiance.

Engaging in equestrian activities along the shore is a captivating opportunity to establish a profound connection with the natural environment as well as the historical context. The guided horseback riding trips provide tourists with the opportunity to traverse unspoiled beaches and verdant landscapes, so providing them a distinct vantage point from which to appreciate the natural splendor of Cozumel. As the sun descends under the horizon, those on horseback are presented with aesthetically pleasing sunset vistas that envelop the water in a luminous, golden hue.

The significance of preparation and respect for nature

When embarking on outdoor experiences in Cozumel, it is essential to emphasize safety, sustainability, and the preservation of the ecosystem. Numerous guided tours and excursions demonstrate a commitment to responsible tourism principles, so guaranteeing that participants have minimum influence on the fragile ecosystems and cultural places.

In summary, the outdoor activities in Cozumel provide a diverse range of experiences suitable for those with various adventurous inclinations. Cozumel offers a range of opportunities for outdoor exploration, including both underwater and land-based activities. These experiences provide insights into the mysteries of the sea and allow individuals to engage with the island's natural environment and cultural heritage. The island's wide range of attractions caters to many preferences, including those seeking exhilarating experiences, serene moments of tranquility, or opportunities for intellectual enrichment. These different options ensure that visitors will be able to construct a collection of lasting memories that will last even after they have departed from the island.

CHAPTER 5

Dining and Cuisine

Cozumel, an idyllic destination renowned for its abundant sunshine and pristine waters, offers more than just visual splendor. It serves as a culinary sanctuary, enticing palates with a rich tapestry of tastes that pay homage to the coastal cuisine of Mexico. The island has a varied gastronomic panorama that reflects its cultural legacy, the abundance of marine resources, and the ingenuity of its culinary experts, ranging from lively street food vendors to sophisticated waterfront establishments. Embark on an exploration of Cozumel's gastronomic landscape, where we will dig into the diverse dining scene and immerse ourselves in the enticing realm of island gastronomy.

A Culinary Fusion: Exploring the Essence of Cozumel's Diverse Cuisine

The culinary landscape of Cozumel is characterized by a rich amalgamation of indigenous Mayan elements, traditional Mexican practices, and diverse foreign influences. The gastronomic options of Cozumel are notably enhanced by the island's geographical position and historical importance as a commercial center, resulting in a combination of tastes.

Regional Culinary Delights: Exquisite Seafood Offerings

Cozumel's cuisine prominently features seafood due to its close proximity to the Caribbean Sea. The island's restaurants showcase the abundance of the ocean in its culinary offerings, with a variety of delectable seafood options ranging from freshly caught fish to juicy shrimp and delicate lobster.

Ceviche is a traditional dish originating from Latin America, particularly popular in coastal regions. It is often made by marinating raw The meal in question serves as a quintessential representation of the fundamental characteristics of Cozumel's seaside gastronomy. Pieces of uncooked fish are immersed in lime juice for a certain period of time, afterwards combined with onions, tomatoes, cilantro, and sometimes chili peppers. The outcome manifests as a revitalizing and tangy amalgamation of tastes that effectively encapsulates the fundamental nature of the ocean.

The dish known as Pescado Tikin Xic is a traditional Mexican seafood preparation.

Pescado tikin xic, a culinary delicacy originating from the Mayan civilization, is the marination of fish with a mixture of achiote paste and other spices. Subsequently, the marinated fish is carefully enveloped in banana leaves and subjected to grilling. The use of banana leaves in the cooking process results in the fish being imbued with a distinct smokey fragrance and a delicate consistency, so producing a culinary creation that both acknowledges customary practices and inventive techniques.

Lobster tails are a culinary delicacy that are highly sought after for their succulent and flavorful meat. The lobster tails found in Cozumel are highly coveted for their culinary appeal, as they are skillfully grilled or broiled to achieve optimal flavor and texture. These delectable crustacean delicacies are often accompanied with a rich garlic butter or a zesty citrus sauce. This opulent indulgence exemplifies the island's capacity to transform even the most basic components into an exceptional culinary creation.

Varieties of Terrestrial Delicacies: Culinary Pleasures from the Land

Seafood is a fundamental element of Cozumel's gastronomy; nonetheless, the island's gastronomic offerings include a diverse range of land-based delicacies that highlight Mexico's abundant agricultural resources.

Tamales are a traditional Mesoamerican dish made of masa (a dough made from corn) that is filled with various ingredients These gastronomic creations, made mostly from maize, are meticulously packed with a diverse array of foods like meats, cheeses, and vegetables. They are then carefully enveloped in banana leaves and subjected to a process of steaming, resulting in an exquisite culinary outcome. Tamales serve as both a representation of Mexico's rich culinary history and a versatile option for convenient consumption, suitable for both light refreshment and substantial sustenance.

Cochinita Pibil is a remarkable culinary creation characterized by the slow-cooking of pork that has been marinated in a blend of achiote and sour orange juice. The marinated pork is then enveloped in banana leaves and cooked until it reaches a soft consistency. The outcome is a cohesive amalgamation of tastes, whereby the achiote imparts a profound and rustic flavour to the meat.

Exploring Dining Experiences: A Spectrum from Street Food to Culinary Refinement

The eating scene in Cozumel has a diverse array of choices that cater to various tastes and financial capacities, including anything from delightful street food vendors to sophisticated waterfront eateries.

Street food stalls are small, mobile food establishments that are often located on the streets or in public spaces. These stalls provide a variety of ready-to-eat food items, such as snacks, meals, and beverages The streets of Cozumel are imbued with a vibrant atmosphere as the scents and tastes of street food sellers permeate the air. Tacos al pastor, a popular dish enjoyed by both residents and tourists, consist of marinated pork that is grilled on a vertical spit and accompanied with pineapple, cilantro, and onions. Equally captivating are elote, a dish consisting of grilled corn on the cob, which is adorned with a delectable mixture of mayonnaise, cheese, and chili powder. This amalgamation of flavors presents a lovely juxtaposition of sweetness and savoriness.

Local eateries refer to dining establishments that are situated inside a specific geographic area, often catering to the local community. These establishments are often characterized by their unique culinary offerings and Cozumel is adorned with a multitude of tiny dining establishments that provide traditional Mexican cuisine prepared in a domestic fashion. These lesser-known establishments provide an opportunity to indulge in genuine tastes within an informal and hospitable environment. These establishments provide a comprehensive experience of Cozumel's culinary culture, with a range of dishes such as robust pozole, a typical soup made with hominy and pork, and chiles rellenos, which are peppers filled with various ingredients.

Waterfront restaurants are dining establishments situated along the edge of a body of water, such as a river, lake, or ocean. These establishments provide patrons the opportunity to enjoy Cozumel's waterfront restaurants provide an elevated dining experience, characterized by breathtaking vistas of the Caribbean Sea. These establishments provide an ideal setting for anyone seeking a romantic evening or a memorable occasion to commemorate. These venues provide exceptional service and innovative culinary dishes that exemplify the progressive development of the island's gastronomy.

Culinary Festivals and Experiences: An Immersive Gastronomic Delight

The culinary events in Cozumel provide a unique chance to immerse oneself in the island's food culture and interact with the dedicated people who contribute to its development.

The Traditional Food Festival in Cozumel is an annual event that celebrates the culinary heritage of the region. The yearly event commemorates the traditional cuisine of Cozumel, highlighting the local gastronomic offerings and indigenous ingredients. Visitors get the opportunity to experience a diverse selection of genuine cuisine, participate in cooking demos, and interact with local chefs who generously impart their culinary knowledge.

Cooking classes are instructional sessions that provide individuals with the opportunity to learn and develop culinary skills and techniques. These classes often include hands-on instruction, where participants are guided by Numerous dining establishments and educational institutions specializing in gastronomy within the locale of Cozumel provide instructional sessions whereby patrons may acquire the knowledge and skills necessary to proficiently craft customary culinary creations, all under the expert tutelage of seasoned chefs. Individuals have the opportunity to fully engage in the practice of crafting tortillas, salsas, and several other culinary delicacies that are representative of Mexican cuisine.

The Art of Mixology: Exploring the Pairing of Spirits

The experience of a gastronomic expedition would be considered incomplete without indulging in the distinctive beverages that Cozumel has to offer. The bartenders on the island possess exceptional expertise in the art of mixology, skillfully crafting drinks that harmonize with the diverse range of tastes found in the local food.

Margaritas are a popular alcoholic beverage that is often made with tequila, lime juice, and orange liqueur. Cozumel's margaritas are a renowned choice, crafted with freshly extracted lime juice, tequila, and a little addition of orange liqueur. Whether consumed over ice or mixed with crushed ice, a margarita serves as an ideal accompaniment to a day dedicated to unwinding or commemorating a special occasion.

Mezcal and tequila tastings are events where participants have the opportunity to sample and evaluate different varieties of mezcal and tequila. Cozumel serves as a prominent entry point to Mexico's esteemed agave beverages. Numerous establishments in the hospitality industry provide opportunities for patrons to engage in tastings, enabling them to delve into the intricacies of tequila and mezcal. These experiences include an exploration of the distinct characteristics inherent in mezcal, such as its smokey undertones, as well as an examination of the varied profiles shown by various expressions of tequila.

The exploration of culinary heritage: An expedition via flavors and customs.

When embarking on a culinary exploration of Cozumel, it is important to appreciate not just the taste profiles but also the narratives associated with every gastronomic creation. The culinary tradition of the island is intricately connected to its historical and cultural background, as well as the dedication of individuals committed to crafting unforgettable dining experiences. The dining scene in Cozumel offers a diverse range of culinary experiences that showcase Mexico's rich gastronomic heritage. From indulging in the finest seafood to exploring traditional recipes, and enjoying expertly created drinks, visitors can expect a sensory feast that celebrates the country's culinary traditions.

In order to fully appreciate the gastronomic offerings of Cozumel, it is recommended that one explores the island's many tastes and indulges in the harmonious culinary symphony that awaits, so allowing the taste buds to experience a delightful dance.

THE END

Made in the USA
Monee, IL
12 October 2023